Before We Stood Tall
From Small Seed to Mighty Tree

Jessica Kulekjian   •   Madeline Kloepper

Kids Can Press

Before we were mighty in the kingdom of trees ...

We gave back to our forest, sending our
seeds on the wind and wisdom underground.

Before our branches sheltered many ...

We remembered the seasons
by tracing the years ...

Before our trunks grew thick ...

line by line.

Our limbs stretched from the shadows, climbing with the giants, who guided the way.

Before we stood tall ...

We clothed ourselves in bark and crowned
ourselves in leaves, waving eagerly at the sun.

Before our twigs transformed ...

Our leaves peeked out at the forest,
catching glimpses of light.

Before we saw the world above ...

Our seeds settled into the earth,
sprouting down,
sprouting out
and sprouting up.

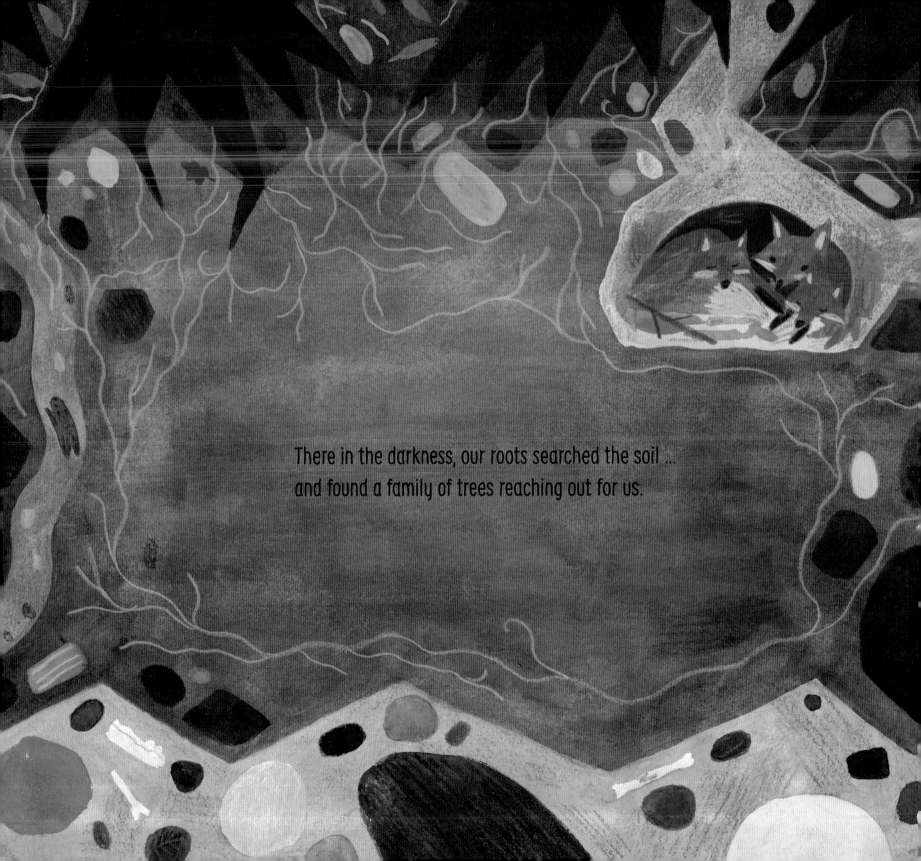

There in the darkness, our roots searched the soil ...
and found a family of trees reaching out for us.

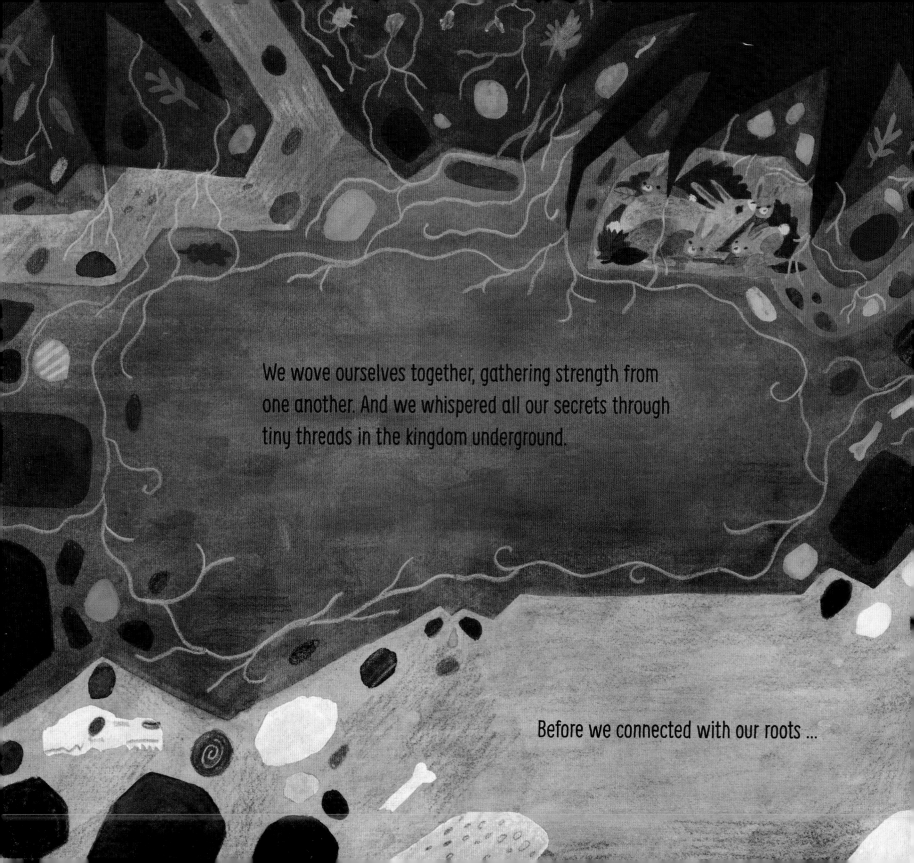

We wove ourselves together, gathering strength from one another. And we whispered all our secrets through tiny threads in the kingdom underground.

Before we connected with our roots ...

We soaked up rain, swelling

out,   out,

We nestled beneath our fallen leaves.

Before our seeds tucked in and waited ...

We greeted the ground,
sinking into its inviting hug.

Before we discovered dirt ...

We twirled through the air, drifting

down,

down,

down...

PLIP!

Before our seeds took flight ...

We dreamed in the branches, hoping to be ...
mighty in the kingdom of trees.

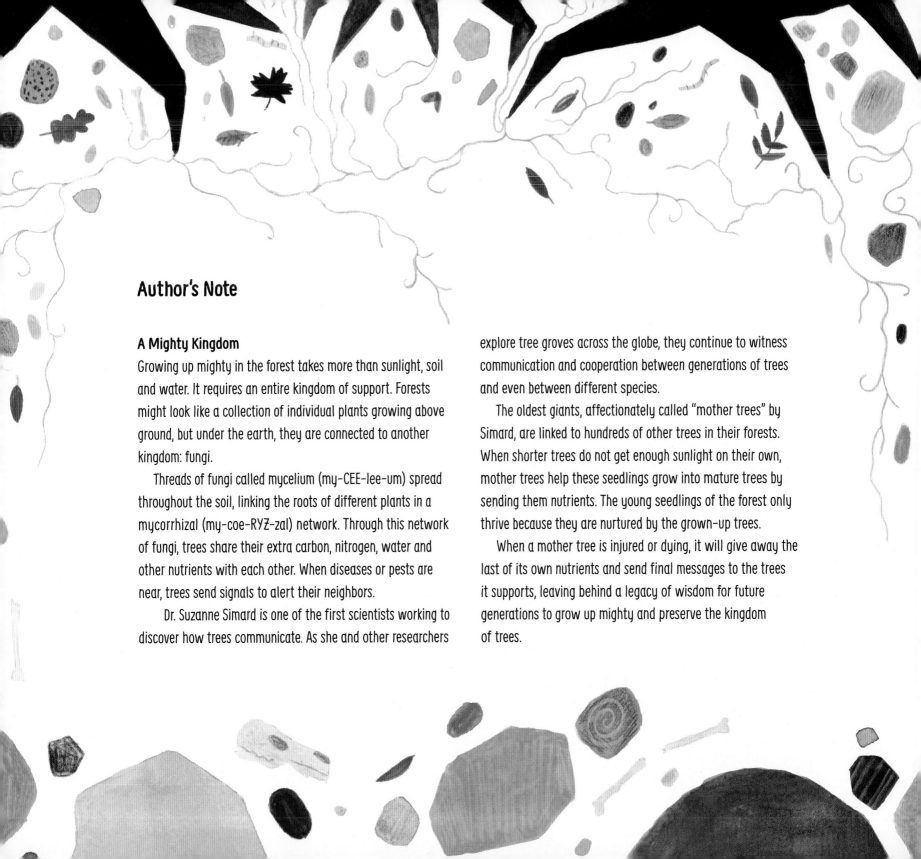

Author's Note

A Mighty Kingdom

Growing up mighty in the forest takes more than sunlight, soil and water. It requires an entire kingdom of support. Forests might look like a collection of individual plants growing above ground, but under the earth, they are connected to another kingdom: fungi.

Threads of fungi called mycelium (my-CEE-lee-um) spread throughout the soil, linking the roots of different plants in a mycorrhizal (my-coe-RYZ-zal) network. Through this network of fungi, trees share their extra carbon, nitrogen, water and other nutrients with each other. When diseases or pests are near, trees send signals to alert their neighbors.

Dr. Suzanne Simard is one of the first scientists working to discover how trees communicate. As she and other researchers explore tree groves across the globe, they continue to witness communication and cooperation between generations of trees and even between different species.

The oldest giants, affectionately called "mother trees" by Simard, are linked to hundreds of other trees in their forests. When shorter trees do not get enough sunlight on their own, mother trees help these seedlings grow into mature trees by sending them nutrients. The young seedlings of the forest only thrive because they are nurtured by the grown-up trees.

When a mother tree is injured or dying, it will give away the last of its own nutrients and send final messages to the trees it supports, leaving behind a legacy of wisdom for future generations to grow up mighty and preserve the kingdom of trees.

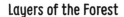
Layers of the Forest

The top of the tree line, called the overstory or canopy, is where the oldest trees stretch their leaves and branches to the sky. Some of the trees that fill in the canopy of the North American hardwood forest (the forest shown in this book) are sugar maple, American beech, white birch, oak and hickory, mixed with softwood conifer trees.

Beneath the treetops is a world called the understory, with a shrub layer, an herb layer and a ground layer. Plants in the shrub layer include witch hazel, viburnums, highbush blueberry, mountain laurel and dogwoods. Below the shrubs grows an herb layer with wildflowers, such as trillium and anemone, that spring to life during the warmer months before the leaves of the trees fill in the canopy above and shade everything below. The ground layer is blanketed with leaves, twigs, grasses and fallen logs. Here, lichens, fungi and mosses do the job of recycling waste into the soil so that the forest can reuse the materials.

Odds of Success

Each seed is packaged inside a tiny covering called a seed coat that protects and nourishes it until it sprouts. Sugar maple trees don't produce seeds until they are about thirty years old. They can produce more than a million in their lifetimes but usually leave behind just one seed that produces a mature tree. For a seed to successfully grow into an adult tree, it must land where there is room to grow toward the sun, receive water and not become a meal for one of the many creatures who live in the forest.

Wildlife

The North American hardwood forest is home to many large animals such as bears, deer, foxes and bobcats, as well as smaller animals such as raccoons, possums and skunks. Common birds include jays, woodpeckers and chickadees, who feed on tree seeds and build nests in the branches. Katydids, walking sticks and caterpillars hide in the leaves, while carpenter bees and termites make their homes in the wood. Creatures such as box turtles, toads, wood frogs and eastern red-spotted newts live on the forest floor. Salamanders and fish swim in the creeks or ponds. Underground, cicadas eat the plant roots.

Sources

Books

Burnie, David. *DK Eyewitness Books: Tree.* NY: DK Publishing, 2015.

Butterworth, Chris. *The Things That I Love about Trees.* Massachusetts: Candlewick Press, 2018.

Hickman, Pamela. *Nature All Around: Trees.* Toronto: Kids Can Press, 2019.

Wohlleben, Peter. *The Hidden Life of Trees.* Vancouver/Berkeley: Greystone Books, 2016.

Films

Dordel, Julia, & Guido Tölke, dirs. *Intelligent Trees.* 2016. Germany: Dorcon Film, 2016. VOD.

Fothergill, Alastair & Mark Linfield, dirs. *Planet Earth.* "Seasonal Forests." Volume 4. 2006. UK: British Broadcasting Corporation, 2006. DVD.

Leven, Russell, dir. *The Magic of Mushrooms.* 2014. UK: British Broadcasting Corporation, 2014. VOD.

Websites

http://www.bbc.com/earth/story/20141111-plants-have-a-hidden-internet

https://www.npr.org/templates/transcript/transcript.php?storyId=509350471

https://www.treesofstrength.org/treefact.htm

https://qz.com/1116991/a-biologist-believes-that-trees-speak-a-language-we-can-learn/

https://www.ted.com/talks/suzanne_simard_how_trees_talk_to_each_other

https://treesforlife.org.uk/into-the-forest/habitats-and-ecology/ecology/mycorrhizas/

For Tyler, Melody and Joy — may love guide you as you grow — J.K.

For Ben and his contagious admiration of forests — M.K.

Acknowledgments

Many people generously shared their expertise to bring this book to life. I'd like to thank Dr. Katherine Waselkov, assistant professor of biology at California State University, Fresno; Dr. John Constable, professor of biology at California State University, Fresno; Ashley Hood, horticulturist and co-owner of Sierra View Nursery; Nathan Warner, Fresno Mycology Society; Jay Kaplan, director, Roaring Brook Nature Center, Canton, CT; Lukas Hyder, forest manager, White Memorial Foundation, Litchfield, CT; and Lawrence Davis-Hollander, ethnobotanist and horticulturist. Finally, my heart is full of gratitude for my creative editor, Kathleen Keenan; my supportive agents, Tracy Marchini and James McGowan; and my encouraging writing community.

Text © 2021 Jessica Kulekjian
Illustrations © 2021 Madeline Kloepper

Published in Canada and the U.S. by Kids Can Press Ltd.
25 Dockside Drive, Toronto, ON M5A 0B5

Kids Can Press is a Corus Entertainment Inc. company

www.kidscanpress.com

The artwork in this book is rendered in watercolor, gouache, colored pencil and finished digitally.
The text is set in Supernett.

Edited by Kathleen Keenan
Designed by Marie Bartholomew

Printed and bound in Dongguan, Guangdong, P.R. China, in 3/2021 by Toppan Leefung

CM 21 0 9 8 7 6 5 4 3 2 1

Library and Archives Canada Cataloguing in Publication

Title: Before we stood tall : from small seed to mighty tree / Jessica Kulekjian ; [illustrated by] Madeline Kloepper.

Names: Kulekjian, Jessica, author. | Kloepper, Madeline, illustrator.

Identifiers: Canadiana 20200364812 | ISBN 9781525303241 (hardcover)

Subjects: LCSH: Trees — Life cycles — Juvenile literature. | LCSH: Trees — Life cycles — Pictorial works — Juvenile literature.

Classification: LCC QK475.8 K85 2021 | DDC j582.16 — dc23

Kids Can Press gratefully acknowledges that the land on which our office is located is the traditional territory of many nations, including the Mississaugas of the Credit, the Anishnabeg, the Chippewa, the Haudenosaunee and the Wendat peoples, and is now home to many diverse First Nations, Inuit and Métis peoples.

We thank the Government of Ontario, through Ontario Creates; the Ontario Arts Council; the Canada Council for the Arts; and the Government of Canada for supporting our publishing activity.